CANADIANS, DON'T GET A MORTGAGE, GET MONEY FOR LIFE

John Geld

Copyright © 2024 John Geld

All rights reserved

The characters and events portrayed in this book are fictitious. Any similarity to real persons, living or dead, is coincidental and not intended by the author.

No part of this book may be reproduced, or stored in a retrieval system, or transmitted in any form or by any means, electronic, mechanical, photocopying, recording, or otherwise, without express written permission of the publisher.

ISBN-13: 9798340956972
ISBN-10: 1477123456

Cover design by: Art Painter
Library of Congress Control Number: 2018675309
Printed in the United States of America

CONTENTS

Title Page
Copyright
Chapter -1: About me   2
Chapter 0: Income   5
Chapter 1: Middle class folks & Mortgage   11
Chapter 2: Bridge loan and when to set closing date   36
Chapter 3: Old folks and mortgages   39
Chapter 4: Young generation that is screwed or 5% down payment nation   45
Chapter 5: Bank loopholes   53
Chapter 6: How mortgage specialists screw you ;)   56
Chapter 7: Skip other chapters if you need to get a mortgage, guide to success   61
Chapter 8: Fu*ck ups   66
Chapter 9: Favor to ask, mortgage specialist to borrowers   68
Chapter 10: If underwriters are reading only   74
Chapter 11: for dear friends from Fraud department, if you are reading this book   76
Chapter 12: If you are going to divorce or remove borrowers from the mortgage   77
Chapter 13: Mortgage for professionals such as Doctors   80

Chapter 14: Scary topic for mortgage specialists, AI take over	83
Chapter 15: For the government and their house crises	85
Epilog	88
About The Author	90
Books By This Author	92

JOHNGELD

Intro

Hello There,

This book is authored by a mortgage specialist with over a decade of experience in the industry. We have encountered all facets of lending. While we will touch on a few interesting points, the primary focus of this book is to assist and guide individuals from various societal levels who are looking to either purchase property or achieve capital stability.

Please note that this book is not intended to provide financial advice or recommendations. The content primarily explores "what if" scenarios and may not apply directly to the reader.

We hope you find this book engaging! We aimed to keep it under 30 pages for an easy read, but it has exceeded that length.

Important Note: All stories are fictional, and all events are entirely made up.

Thank you!

CHAPTER -1: ABOUT ME

Hello, dear reader!

Before you dive into this book, please note that it is not intended to provide professional advice. Instead, it offers opinions on current mortgages in Canada, including insights on obtaining a mortgage and what specialists look for.

Feel free to skip the first chapter, as it's a biography about me—a random guy. The important information starts in the subsequent chapters. Additionally, I will be publishing a separate book detailing my experiences as a mortgage specialist, styled similarly to "Better Call Saul." Fingers crossed!

I began my career as a mortgage specialist in December 2010, right after passing the exam. The field was simpler back then, but the core concepts remain unchanged. My older brother, already a mortgage specialist at the bank, introduced me to the profession.

While studying at university, I pursued a career in financial lending. Admittedly, it wasn't easy starting out on my own with no mentor or portfolio to inherit. I had to work hard to build my career. Despite the lack of guidance, I didn't give up. I devised a strategy involving lectures and distributing flyers. I used my last bit of OSAP funds to print those flyers, and though it was tough—especially in the cold winter—I persevered. I'd distribute between 100 to 300 flyers a day, hoping to attract clients. Instagram was in its early stages, and Google Ads was becoming popular. After a few weeks, some clients began to reach out.

My advertising initially focused on second private mortgages, which were less than ideal. I disliked dealing with these mortgages, but they were profitable. My boss at the time encouraged me to focus on them, promising substantial earnings. For example, on a $40K loan, a $55K second private loan could result in significant fees. Though it seemed lucrative, it was not a sustainable or ethical practice. I eventually moved away from these types of loans.

One memorable experience involved a client whom we promised significant benefits, only for them to face high fees and challenges. The reality was often disappointing, with clients sometimes ending up in worse financial situations. Debt management and financial literacy were crucial, and unfortunately, many clients struggled with both.

Once we gathered all necessary documents and completed the appraisal—often challenging outside the GTA—we sought investors for the loan. The process involved significant negotiation and documentation, and fees were a contentious issue. I had to balance transparency with maintaining client trust.

In one particularly amusing incident, my partner and I, dressed in suits and armed with energy drinks, faced an unusual situation where a pen attack occurred during a document-signing meeting. Despite such challenges, we continued to push forward.

Business gradually improved, and my partner and I rented a small office in the Barrie region. However, personal circumstances forced me to leave university and focus on supporting my family.

At one point, my partner and I decided to work from a coffee shop, adapting to a changing environment. During this time, I met my future manager, who left a business card and encouraged me to reach out. Initially hesitant, I eventually took the offer to become a mortgage advisor, shifting away from private mortgages and learning new lending programs.

With my brother's encouragement, I joined a bank as a mortgage specialist in 2013. The transition was eye-opening, providing insight into the corporate world and the complexities of mortgage lending. Although I faced many challenges, I eventually became a top producer. My branch, conveniently located near home, was well-suited to serve the self-employed community.

However, by the end of 2017, regulatory changes and internal issues led to a contraction in the bank's mortgage lending. My attempts to propose solutions were unacknowledged, leading me to seek opportunities elsewhere.

In January 2017, I left the bank and returned to the brokerage world, where I had to renew my mortgage agent license and obtain a broker license. That year was challenging but rewarding, as I managed a team of 12 mortgage specialists and navigated the impacts of new regulations on the market.

Despite my efforts, the broker world often felt adversarial, with lenders perceiving brokers as untrustworthy. Frustrated, I eventually applied to other banks and secured a position with a supportive manager.

I plan to write a book revealing the most intriguing and hidden aspects of the mortgage lending industry, inspired by the "Better Call Saul" style. Stay tuned for more!

Happy reading!

CHAPTER 0: INCOME

This chapter aims to shed light on income verification, highlighting a paradox where individuals may believe they have substantial income, but banks might see it differently. It's an ironic situation, but it's true. To make matters more complex, if you purchased a property before 2010, you weren't required to provide as detailed income documentation as you are now. While Generation Z must navigate these stricter requirements creatively, understanding the key aspects of income verification is crucial. We'll focus on the primary income categories: employed and self-employed. In simple words, bank only likes employed people or people whose income can be confirmed. Also, we never use line 150 as your income as it does not tell us much but just a final summed up income from different source of income.

Employed Income

For those who are employed, confirming income is generally straightforward. Banks typically require a letter of employment, pay stubs, bank deposits, and sometimes T4 slips. We use these documents to calculate your gross income for our ratio assessments, which we'll cover in the next chapter.

Fixed vs. Variable Income

- **Fixed Income**: Individuals with a fixed annual salary or hourly rate with guaranteed hours are easier to verify.
- **Variable Income:** If your income varies, such as with nurses or part-time workers, we use the average income from the past two years. We may ask for T4 slips or T1

General forms with a Notice of Assessment (NOA). If your current year-to-date pay stub shows consistent earnings with your last T4 slip, we prefer using that. If your current year's income is less than the previous T4, we rely on the T4 slips from the past two years along with a letter of employment and, if needed, bank statements.

Bonuses and Overtime

For those with bonuses or overtime pay. We review your T4 slips from previous years to determine how much bonus or overtime income can be included to mitigate ratios.

Rental and Other Income

- **Rental Income**: Banks often require T1 General forms with the NOA or a lease agreement and bank statements showing rental deposits. Be mindful that some underwriters might not understand deductions on rental income in T1 general, which could complicate the process.
- **Dividend Income**: We review T1 General forms and NOA from the last two years, and also check business registration and T2 forms to assess the company's performance and future income potential.

Important Points

- **Line 150 on T1 General**: This line totals all income sources and is not typically used for verification. We focus on specific lines that reflect consistent income.
- **Child Support Benefits**: These are generally acceptable as income, requiring NOA Child Support Benefit and two months of bank statements. A birth certificate may be required to confirm eligibility based on age limits.
- **Investments**: Investment income needs to be confirmed through investment statements and T1 General forms with NOA.

Self-Employed Income

Self-employed income verification is more complex. A banks (traditional banks) may be cautious, while B banks (alternative lenders) are more flexible but charge higher interest rates and fees. B lenders require extensive documentation, such as 12-month business bank statements to confirm annual income.

Required Documents:

- **Sole Proprietors**: T1 General, NOA, business registration, and business bank statements.
- **Incorporated Businesses**: Articles of Incorporation, business financial statements for the last two years, and business bank statements.

As part of the mortgage application process, self-employed individuals often face challenges when it comes to income verification. While it is common for self-employed individuals to show a high gross income and lower net profit, banks typically assess the net profit for lending purposes. There are specific lines on the T1 General tax form that we can consider as income, and it's crucial that this income remains consistent over the next two years.

For instance, if your corporation pays you a salary in one year, we would use Line 101, and if it pays you dividends the next year, we would refer to Line 120 on the T1 General. Although it can be inconvenient for mortgage specialists, it is possible to average the income over two years using Line 101 and Line 120. However, we will need to explain any changes to the underwriters.

Complications arise when different lines are used, such as Line 139 in one year and Line 120 in another. This can indicate a shift from operating as a sole proprietor to incorporation, which can confuse underwriters, especially those who may not be familiar with the intricacies of self-employment income. We often find ourselves explaining these nuances to younger underwriters, which can delay the process.

It's important to note that the income lines considered by banks may vary, so it's advisable to consult with your mortgage specialist to determine which lines they will accept. Ideally, consistent income on the same line over the past two years is preferred. For example, if you're using Line 101 to pay yourself a salary, we need two years of salary income. If you're using dividend income (Line 120), or business/professional income, again, we require a two-year income history for consideration."

Another important point to consider is that this year's income tax will be based on the individual lines in the T1 General, not on Line 150. Line 150 simply reflects the sum of all income sources. Ideally, your income on specific lines, such as Line 101 or Line 139, should be at least the same or higher than the previous year. If your income on these lines is lower than last year, we will be forced to use only the current year's income, and we cannot average it over two years. This will result in a lower income figure in our calculations, ultimately reducing the loan amount for which you qualify.

Banks will question why the client's income is lower, raising concerns about potential financial issues. If you are planning to buy a property or refinance, it's essential to start reflecting this income on your tax returns. Some people believe they can outsmart the system by working with mortgage specialists who offer creative solutions, but this often comes at a cost—whether through under-the-table fees or higher interest rates. In the end, you will pay either way, so it's preferable to claim more income on your taxes rather than incur higher fees or interest rates.

In my upcoming book, I will delve into the growing issue of income and mortgage fraud, as it has become increasingly sophisticated with people seeking loans. My best advice is to avoid mortgage specialists who charge fees to help you qualify by artificially inflating your income. It's simply not worth it. Not everything is for everyone, but if you're serious about buying property, make an appointment with a professional and work on a plan to achieve your goals.

This is especially important in the current market, where both interest rates and qualification rates are high, making it difficult for many people to qualify based on their actual income. Unfortunately, some individuals fall into the trap of working with specialists who promise special services for a fee. I often find myself stepping in at the last minute when the closing date is fast approaching and no extension is allowed. These clients were often falsely assured that everything was fine, only to find out at the last minute that fraudulent documents were caught, leaving them in a bind.

It's disheartening that some mortgage specialists continue to deceive clients by promising solutions that won't work. They fail to realize that this will only bring more problematic cases in the future. Instead of misleading clients, it's better to refer them to alternative lenders (B lenders) if their situation warrants it."

Final Thoughts

Always ensure your income tax documents are accurate and reflect true income. Attempting to manipulate documents can lead to complications and higher costs in the long run. It's better to work with a knowledgeable mortgage specialist who can guide you through the process honestly. Avoid mortgage specialists who offer to manipulate documents for a fee, as this can lead to more problems down the line.

In my next book, I'll explore the complexities of income and mortgage fraud in greater detail. For now, remember that honesty and transparency are key in securing a mortgage.

And to the fraud department, if you're reading this, rest assured this is all fictional, crafted to engage readers and support my next book.

Happy reading!

CHAPTER 1: MIDDLE CLASS FOLKS & MORTGAGE

I hate to break it to you, but if the government continues on its current course, many of us will be left behind, unable to participate in the housing market. To put things into perspective, my parents once received a semi-detached, two-story home with balconies, along with half an acre of land that included a barn, garage, storage space, a sauna, and a large plot for growing agricultural produce—all provided by the government, for free. This was also true for my grandparents, my uncle, and others. They didn't need a mortgage because the government prioritized people's well-being over making a profit. The most remarkable part, It was theirs, outright—they held the title. If you're wondering where this was, it was the USSR, where there was no room for capitalists to profit from hardworking people through mortgage interest.

Fast forward to 2024, and we are witnessing a troubling decline in the number of middle-class families owning property. This should be a major concern, as the government appears to be doing little to prevent further damage to society. If you're part of the middle class in Canada and you currently own a property, consider yourself fortunate. In today's market, owning a home is increasingly rare, and if you've managed to achieve this, it's a significant accomplishment.

However, simply owning property is not enough. It's crucial that you manage your finances carefully to avoid losing it. Many homeowners are surprised by how easily they can lose their only property due to mismanaged debt. A significant number of people found themselves in this situation after the SARS-COV-2 pandemic, with many forced to sell their primary residence due to financial strain. Once again, the government showed little concern for the well-being of its people.

So, if you currently own a property—whether it's a house or a condominium—it's important to analyze your situation carefully, especially regarding borrowing. Whether you have high or low levels of debt, now is the time to take a closer look at your financial standing and make sure you're protecting your assets. Let's start analyzing.

Assuming you own a house with significant debt, this means your property has little or no equity that can be leveraged. Perhaps you refinanced the property to access additional funds, such as to purchase a new car—unless it was needed for work, this is typically a poor financial decision. Alternatively, you may have a second or third private mortgage that is approaching its maturity date and needs to be paid off.

If you only have one mortgage, I recommend waiting for the market to grow before accessing your equity. When the market value increases, you can use that opportunity to take out equity at a more favorable time. Ideally, your first step should be to contact your current lender, who holds the primary mortgage, and inquire about the possibility of securing a line of credit. If you're looking for better terms, you may want to explore other banks, as another institution might offer more competitive refinancing options.

Typically, if you are employed and earning a good income, refinancing should not be an issue. Banks often compete by offering better rates and incentives for refinancing. The key strategy is to wait for the market value to increase. Once your loan-to-value ratio is below 70%—meaning your current loan balance is less than 70% of the property's market value—you may have up to 10% equity to withdraw for future investments.

Keep in mind that this process may take time and will vary depending on the location of your property. If you're looking to maximize your equity, consider purchasing property closer to major cities if buying within the city limits is not feasible. Houses tend to appreciate faster and gain more equity than condominiums. When you do access your equity, focus on investing those funds rather than paying off existing debts like credit cards, which can be managed over time.

To summarize, if your property is heavily leveraged, it's important to wait for the market to improve before accessing equity. Condominiums typically appreciate more slowly than houses, so the timeline may be longer for those types of properties. It's also wise to consult specialists who can help you assess your income and determine whether you need to increase it in order to refinance your entire debt or access equity as the property value grows.

Now, if you have a property with substantial equity and minimal debt, here's what you should consider. It's often advantageous to get a mortgage with an attached line of credit, though not everyone will qualify for this option. If you already have a mortgage, start by checking whether your current interest rate is better or worse compared to the current market rates. If your rate is higher and banks are offering better rates, find out what your penalty would be for breaking the mortgage. By comparing the penalty with your monthly principal and interest payments, you can determine if refinancing is worthwhile. You can ask a mortgage specialist to calculate this for you, or you can use an online mortgage calculator with an amortization schedule to get a rough estimate.

Additionally, some banks offer cash-back promotions that cover costs like appraisal fees, legal fees, and even penalties in certain cases. So, if your mortgage term is nearing its end, or if more favorable terms are available, it might be worth refinancing. While it's a good idea to check other banks, staying with your current lender can simplify the process if you're not seeking additional funds. In that case, the bank will often auto-renew your mortgage. However, exploring other banks may uncover cash-back offers that could offset the costs of switching, such as appraisal, legal, and discharge fees.

Some banks offer mortgage products that convert a portion of your principal payments into a line of credit. These products go by different names but function similarly: with each principal payment, the balance available on your line of credit increases. While this option may be harder to qualify for, it offers flexibility by allowing you to access funds later if needed without withdrawing money immediately.

If the penalty for breaking your mortgage or the current rate is too attractive to pass up, you should consider a secured line of credit. It's generally more advantageous to get the secured line with the same bank that holds your first mortgage. For instance, if you have a mortgage with TD Bank, it's better to get a secured line of credit with TD as well, since they can offer up to 80% loan-to-value (LTV), whereas other banks may only provide up to 65% LTV. To avoid confusion, if your mortgage is with BMO, it's best to get a line of credit with BMO. If you try to get one with TD instead, they will only offer up to 65% LTV.

Certainly! Here's a more polished and professional version of the text:

You might think that getting a line of credit or refinancing your mortgage is a straightforward way to access funds, but it's not as easy as it seems. Each year, banks tighten their lending rules and regulations, making it increasingly difficult to get loan approvals. This forces mortgage specialists to become more creative in navigating the system.

In 2024, for instance, with the prime rate sitting at 6.45%, qualifying for a loan has become even more challenging. If you want to borrow $500,000, you now need a household income of $100,000. Before these recent changes, $100,000 in income could have qualified you for a mortgage of up to $800,000, but little has been done to address this shift.

For more details on the required documentation and how we review loan applications, refer to Chapter 0, which provides a comprehensive overview.

Congratulations on your approval! Now that you have access to the funds, here's what to expect next. A good mortgage specialist will send a detailed email to you, your lawyer (if one is involved), and the branch representative responsible for signing the bank documents. They will review all the details and ensure that everything is in order. After the final meeting, you can expect a proper farewell email, often accompanied by a small token of appreciation for your business.

If you've completed a mortgage-only refinance, it's important not to finalize the deal or release the funds until you have a clear plan for where you will invest the money. If your mortgage converts into a line of credit, you should proceed by completing the funding with the mortgage balance you need, while keeping the line of credit open for future use.

One important note: when you withdraw money from the line of credit portion, you can convert those funds into mini-mortgages with fixed payments that reduce the principal. Otherwise, you will continue paying interest without making any progress toward paying down the balance. If you've received just a line of credit, you're in a good position—simply activate it and keep it available for when you need it."

While I'm not giving specific financial advice, here are a few strategies I would personally consider when dealing with extra funds. A simple approach would be to invest in ETFs within a joint TFSA account, which offers a degree of security. However, I would also consider private lending. For beginners, I recommend investing in a Mortgage Investment Corporation (MIC) or working closely with your mortgage broker.

A MIC is a corporation that pays you interest on the money you lend to them. They typically charge borrowers around 12% interest, while paying investors about 8%, with the difference retained by the MIC. However, be cautious, as there are fraudulent MICs, and some investors have lost all their money. Keep in mind that any investment carries risk.

Personally, I prefer to be a private lender. I typically charge 11% interest with an additional 1% lender fee, which would result in a borrower paying me around $450 per month on a $50,000 loan. Given the current line of credit interest rate as of July 2024 is prime minus 0.5%, or 7.20%, and I collect 11%, the difference is 3.80%. Not a bad margin. As interest rates are projected to drop further by the central bank, both later in 2024 and into 2025, line of credit payments will decrease, and profits could increase. This method can be more straightforward and profitable, though it does involve some effort.

Another option I would consider is purchasing an investment property. Real estate is a solid hedge against inflation, as your investment doesn't depreciate in value the way cash can. Some may argue that there are easier and more flexible ways to invest, such as in financial products that offer quick liquidity and can help avoid issues like CRA taxation. However, buying investment properties—particularly through a holding company—offers long-term security. We'll cover holding companies later in the book.

Once you've accessed funds from your property, consider investing in private lending, some in a bank ETF, and reserve the rest for an investment property. Instead of a single-family home, opt for a duplex or fourplex. Some banks can finance up to an eight-unit property, though these tend to come at a premium. Owning multiple properties, as opposed to just one, can make retirement easier. As we'll explore in Chapter 3, owning more than one property gives you more financial freedom and flexibility, allowing you to preserve your primary residence.

For example, I own both a primary residence and several investment properties. When the time comes and I feel like indulging or preparing to pass my assets to the next generation, I have the option to either enjoy the fruits of my investments or leave them as a legacy for my children.

Buying an investment property may seem exciting and rewarding—at least on paper. In reality, it can be a challenging process, so proceed with caution.

First and foremost, always get pre-approval before you begin searching for a property. Don't start your search without securing financing first. For details on the necessary documents and how to get started, refer to Chapter 0. Once you're pre-approved and have found a suitable investment property, I recommend purchasing it under a holding corporation.

To clarify, this advice isn't about pushing you into buying another property for the sake of commission—trust me, it's a hassle on our end, too. Instead, this is about helping you achieve financial stability and long-term happiness. With the current housing crisis in Toronto, Ontario, and no immediate solutions from the government, the demand for rental properties will remain high for the next 5 to 10 years. Don't worry—communism isn't coming to Canada anytime soon, at least not for the next 300 years, and we'll discuss this more in my upcoming book. For those who know their history, you'll understand that even feudalism didn't last forever.

Now, back to the investment property. Once you've bought it, the next step is to start renting it out. While the process can be complex, it's ultimately worth it. You have the option to either sell the property later for a profit or keep it, pass it down to your children, and use the rental income to pay down any borrowed funds from your primary residence. Property values will continue to appreciate over time, so you need to decide your strategy: you can either invest in a high-end property, which requires substantial capital to maintain, or choose a more modest duplex or fourplex and maximize its value over time.

In the long run, investing in real estate can provide a solid financial foundation—just be prepared for the challenges along the way.

Why Buy Under a Holding Corporation?

There are two key reasons to consider buying property under a holding corporation, although many mortgage specialists may not like me revealing this lesser-known strategy—nothing personal, but I want this book to be informative and widely read.

When you purchase either a primary or investment property under a numbered holding corporation, it can offer certain advantages. One important point to note: it's generally advised to set up a separate corporation for each property.

If you buy your primary residence under a holding corporation, the general idea is that you intend to keep the property long-term and eventually pass it on to your children. However, if you plan to sell the property later—whether it's your primary residence or an investment property—you will be subject to double taxation. This is a significant consideration.

So, if selling the property is part of your future plan, I strongly advise against purchasing it through a numbered holding corporation. The tax implications make it less advantageous for property sales, particularly when you could otherwise avoid the extra tax burden by holding the property personally.

If you plan to keep a property long-term and pass it on to your children, there are several compelling reasons to purchase under a holding corporation. Here's why this strategy can be beneficial:

- **Privacy and Credit Reporting:** When you buy a property through a holding corporation, each property should be placed in a separate corporation. This approach helps with privacy, as the property is registered under the corporation's name, not yours personally. Consequently, other banks won't see these properties on your personal credit report. This can be advantageous if you seek additional financing, as other lenders won't be aware of your existing property holdings. Note that after this book is published, it might take 2 to 5 years before banks adjust their systems to counter this strategy, so readers should act sooner rather than later.

- **Tax Benefits:** Another significant advantage of using a holding corporation is related to taxation. Rental income generated by properties held in a corporation does not impact your personal income tax bracket. This means you pay less tax to the Canada Revenue Agency (CRA), which can be particularly beneficial given Canada's high income tax rates. A holding corporation allows you to keep your personal tax bracket unaffected while the corporation pays a lower tax rate—typically around 12% on profits, depending on the province. Additionally, the corporation can write off various expenses related to the property, further optimizing your tax situation.

By managing properties through a holding corporation, you can mitigate personal tax liabilities and maintain a favorable credit profile, making it a strategic choice for long-term property management and investment.

Another Advantage of Holding Corporations: Succession Planning

One notable benefit of using a holding corporation is its efficiency in succession planning. When you purchase a property through a holding corporation and you are the sole director, this structure can simplify matters for your heirs.

Upon your passing—something everyone must face eventually—your investment property will be transferred to your family or heirs. The bank will first inquire whether your heirs intend to transfer the property into their names or sell it. If they choose to keep it, they will need to qualify for the property, which is often a challenge. In approximately 70% of cases, heirs may struggle with affordability and may end up selling the property within six months. If they cannot manage the property, the bank may take further action.

Moreover, the Canada Revenue Agency (CRA) will consider the property as an inheritance, which means taxes may be applicable either when the title is transferred or when the property is sold. This can create an additional financial burden.

However, if the property is held under a holding corporation, the process is more straightforward. You simply need to assign a new director, such as a family member or estate representative. This transfer doesn't require re-applying for the mortgage or paying additional taxes, making it a smoother transition.

The ultimate goal is to strategically manage your properties over time. By the age of 60, you can remortgage properties, acquire additional ones, pay down existing mortgages, and eventually pass these assets on to your children. This approach provides them with a stronger financial foundation and simplifies the inheritance process.

A common issue arises when children inherit their parents' real estate portfolios: they may lack the work ethic or responsibility needed to manage these assets effectively. This is why it's important to establish a family trust to clearly define ownership and management of the holding corporation's assets.

In Canada, there is a segment of the population where individuals rely on inherited investment properties for income without actively working or paying taxes. This situation has prompted the Canadian government to implement new regulations affecting banks and investment properties.

It's crucial to act quickly and strategically. Similar to regulations on firearm ownership, which aim to address broader societal concerns, financial regulations are evolving to address the management of inherited wealth. The goal is to ensure responsible handling of assets and prevent misuse.

The government's approach to regulating handgun sales, driven by concerns over rising crime rates, reflects a broader policy strategy. The intent behind such regulations is often to reduce the availability of firearms, thereby aiming to decrease overall crime and violence. However, it is important to recognize that responsible firearm owners typically do not intend to engage in criminal activities or sell firearms to criminals.

The underlying concern may be to limit the potential for armed resistance against government authority. Historically, the presence of firearms has played a role in enabling citizens to challenge or influence government policies. By restricting access to firearms, the government may seek to minimize this potential and maintain public order.

By setting up a family trust, you can manage the transition of assets more effectively and ensure that the next generation is prepared to handle these responsibilities. Taking this step now will help avoid complications in the future and ensure that your estate is managed according to your wishes.

If you are a middle-class family currently renting, here is what you need to consider to become a real estate investor. The first question you must ask yourself is whether this is truly what you want.

Remember that property owners often experience greater satisfaction, as they have the freedom to make modifications to their property, such as drilling holes or purchasing furniture that suits their tastes. In contrast, renters must be cautious and considerate of the property they are renting, always mindful of its condition.

If you decide to pursue real estate investment, there are several pathways to achieve this goal. However, it's important to acknowledge that the current Canadian government policies have made it increasingly challenging for middle-class families to achieve home ownership.

If you are a middle-class individual currently renting, especially if you are on your own, it can be challenging, but don't lose hope. If you are living with your parents, consider setting aside a portion of your income each month to start investing. Connect your investments to your Tax-Free Savings Account (TFSA), as this can maximize your returns. While some investments may incur losses, they represent a risk that could accelerate your path to achieving your financial goals. Prioritize paying yourself first and handle credit card payments and loans afterwards. This strategy can help you reach your objectives more quickly.

However, be cautious not to damage your credit by neglecting payments entirely. Maintain minimal payments and keep your credit utilization below 80% of your limit to avoid significant drops in your credit score.

If moving back in with your parents for six months is not an option, consider alternatives like those seen in successful cases where individuals saved for a down payment by ceasing rent payments. As an investor and landlord, I understand that while this may provide temporary financial relief, it can lead to legal consequences, including court action. If you choose this route, it is essential to inform your landlord and plan to repay the rent owed. Failing to do so could result in significant repercussions, including legal action, frozen bank accounts, and difficulties in managing future mortgage payments. Remember, ethical behavior is crucial, as unresolved disputes with landlords can have lasting negative effects on your financial well-being and personal life.

If you start saving $300 per month, that amounts to $3,600 per year or $18,000 over the next five years. With this, you may have an opportunity to invest in a small condominium as a starting point. For a breakdown of the associated costs, refer to the next section.

In Ontario, some builders allow a 5% down payment on pre-construction properties. Payment options may include lump sum or monthly installments. While this can be a good starting point, exercise caution, as these properties often appreciate in value more slowly. Focus on purchasing one-bedroom condos priced under $500,000.

If you're considering purchasing a $500,000 condo, whether pre-construction or resale, you'll need to earn an annual income of $100,000 if you're putting down 5%, at least in 2024. In 2025, if interest rates decline, a lower income requirement may apply. This is because both the bank and mortgage insurance companies will assess your application. While the bank may be willing to lend, mortgage insurers have stricter criteria.

A 5% down payment on a $500,000 property is $25,000. If you're not paying rent or living with your parents, aim to save approximately $2,000 per month over the next year. This goal is achievable with discipline.

One advantage of purchasing a pre-construction property is the potential for value appreciation, allowing you to assign (sell) the contract before the final closing. This way, you can recover your initial deposit and make a profit without needing to secure a mortgage.

However, finding properties with a 5% down payment requirement can be challenging, though they do exist. Most builder projects require a 20% down payment, but some of these may offer assignment options as well. If you opt to buy an existing property, you'll likely only be able to purchase a condominium with a 5% down payment.

When considering an investment property, always evaluate the area's potential for rental income and future appreciation. Look for locations that will benefit from new transit developments, such as expansions by the Toronto Transit Commission (TTC), which operates the city's subway, streetcars, and buses.

Additionally, pay attention to condominium fees. Older buildings tend to have higher fees, so keep that in mind when making your decision.

If you're reading this in 2024, you may be fortunate enough to secure your first investment condominium. However, it's important to note that the government has not handled the real estate sector effectively. Many investors in condominiums may face losses and could be looking to liquidate their properties. This could present a unique buying opportunity for savvy investors.

You're welcome.

If you have a large family, this can be a key to financial survival, yet government policies often seem to work against the strengthening of families. A strong, supportive family can help you achieve a great deal, but if you're on your own, it may take longer and be more difficult to reach your goals.

Interestingly, when interest rates were low, the birth rate increased, but with today's high interest rates and housing affordability issues, many people are reconsidering whether they can afford to have children, as raising a family in Canada has become increasingly expensive. The government offers minimal support to young families, instead prioritizing foreign aid and sending resources abroad, when it should be focusing on addressing domestic issues like housing and family welfare.

While you work on saving for your down payment, it's crucial to focus on two additional factors: your income and your credit. In 2024, mortgage qualifications are based on the interest rate plus 2%, due to the government's stress test requirements. You must pass the stress test before being considered eligible for a mortgage.

Before 2016, buyers with a 5% down payment could qualify for a mortgage using a five-year fixed rate, which was around 3%, making it much easier for people to secure financing. However, since the summer of 2016, the stress test has drastically impacted first-time buyers, requiring them to qualify under stricter conditions, regardless of whether they have a 5% or 25% down payment.

Some argue that the stress test was intended to stabilize the housing market, but mortgage specialists were not consulted, and the results speak for themselves. As we see in 2024, the market remains overheated, and people are facing greater challenges than before. The stress test failed to solve the underlying issues, yet the government seems indifferent to the struggles of ordinary people.

Returning to the current situation, in 2024, the stress test requires you to qualify at the market rate plus 2%. As of summer 2024, the lowest available three-year fixed non-insured rate is 5.24%, meaning you need to qualify at 7.24%. This qualifying rate is expected to drop a couple of times—once more in 2024 and again in 2025.

While this prediction may change, it offers a useful guideline for future planning. When calculating your potential mortgage, always take the current market rate and add 2%. For example, if you're making a 5% down payment, your household income should be around $100,000 annually to qualify.

Banks use specific formulas to determine whether you qualify for a mortgage, known as GDS (Gross Debt Service) and TDS (Total Debt Service) ratios. GDS includes your qualifying monthly mortgage payment (calculated using the rate plus 2%), heating costs, property taxes, and condominium fees if applicable. This total is divided by your income. Most banks have standard limits of 42% for GDS and 44% for TDS, though some offer more flexible ratios, providing clients with greater financial leeway. BMO bank has more flexibility.

TDS is the total of all your debt payments divided by your income. This includes your GDS, plus any monthly credit and car loan payments. To optimize your chances, avoid leasing or financing a car in your personal name, as doing so under a business name excludes it from the bank's calculations.

When purchasing a property with less than a 20% down payment, both the bank and mortgage insurers will review your file. If your credit (beacon) score is below 680, your GDS and TDS ratios are limited to 36% and 39%, respectively. However, if your score is above 680, you may qualify for the more favorable 39% GDS and 42% TDS ratios, increasing your chances of securing the right mortgage amount.

For a detailed breakdown of what is considered income by banks, please refer to Chapter 0. This is an extensive topic, and many people who believe they have sufficient income may not even qualify for a credit card in the eyes of the bank.

Now that you understand the importance of income, it's clear that the higher your income, the better your chances of securing the right property. However, it's essential not to overextend yourself when purchasing a home. Earning $100K per year is a solid achievement and means you can likely save for a down payment, but many middle-class individuals are only now reaching this income level, often while carrying significant debt.

This reality makes it difficult for many Canadians to buy property at the moment, but rest assured, they will have the opportunity to do so at some point in their lives.

Credit score is another crucial factor when applying for a mortgage. If your beacon score is below 600, there's a 90% chance that A lenders (major banks) will decline your application unless you have a strong justification. At this point, B lenders come into play, but they typically offer higher interest rates, lender fees, and additional costs. It's in your best interest to maintain a good credit score.

A lower credit score decreases the likelihood that either a bank or an insurance company will approve your application. To avoid this, make sure to keep up with minimal payments and keep your credit balances below 80% of their limits to prevent your score from dropping further.

If you're planning to buy a property, don't focus solely on paying off your credit cards first. Instead, prioritize setting aside money for your down payment, while maintaining minimal payments on your credit cards. This is because, when you eventually purchase a property and see its value grow over the next 2-3 years, you'll have more resources to pay off those balances. Paying off high-interest debt through lump sums could take years, so managing it strategically is key.

One final note: if your beacon score is below 600 and you have less than 20% for a down payment, it's unlikely your mortgage application will be considered. In such cases, it's essential to consult with a mortgage specialist before proceeding.

Typically, Canadians don't earn very high incomes, and this is partly due to the policies of the Canadian government. They raise taxes without developing the infrastructure needed for industries like mining or manufacturing. Instead, they issue mining licenses and offer tax breaks to operators, while continuously borrowing money and distributing it, which fuels inflation and raises the cost of living. If you're watching this, Canadian government, it's time to start planning your exit strategy.

Canadians often remain stagnant with a bachelor's degree or diploma, but lifelong learning is crucial for growth. You should always be striving to improve, ideally by taking at least one course per semester. Some might object, saying they don't have the money or the time. However, consider this: I consistently further my education, not just for financial gain, but for personal development.

For adults, there's also OSAP, the Ontario Student Assistance Program, which provides student loans for university or college courses. While funding may not be available for all programs, there are still options that allow you to continue learning. Time is another barrier many people cite. It's true that hard-working middle-class Canadians may struggle to find the time, but many others spend countless hours on social media or watching TV. Imagine how much of that time could be redirected toward personal growth, enabling you to earn more, take nicer vacations, or buy a better car. Taking just 2 or 3 courses per semester is enough to gradually advance and develop new skills.

Consider the approach of the USSR, which focused on human development, allowing the government to take care of day-to-day responsibilities so people could innovate. This led to significant achievements like sending the first human to space, developing nuclear technologies, and creating vaccines. The USSR was a nation of readers, focusing on intellectual growth, unlike Canada today, where many people struggle just to pay their bills.

Sadly, the USSR's system was also abused, which contributed to its downfall. Today, Canada is not known for excelling in science or math Olympiads. Instead, countries like China, Russia, and India consistently dominate, along with the U.S. Interestingly, many top American competitors are of Chinese, Russian, or Indian descent. Meanwhile, Canada has fallen behind intellectually. We don't rank highly in terms of advanced degrees or book readership, but we lead in screen time on social media, and cannabis stores seem to be on every corner.

It's hard not to see this as intentional. Governments may encourage such trends to win elections and make people less intellectually engaged. Legalized cannabis consumption leads to mental degradation over time, which results in a less informed, more easily controlled population—a goal that appears convenient for those in power.

Now, returning to the topic of mortgage rates and terms, and how to choose the right one. Typically, if you put down less than 20%, you are limited to a 25-year amortization period. However, if you can put down more than 20%, you may qualify for a 30-year amortization. Some banks even offer 35 to 40-year options, though these are more difficult to obtain. Extending the amortization period results in lower monthly payments, but you end up paying more in interest over time. It's important to remember that banks profit significantly during the first five years of your mortgage.

There is also a new program for first-time buyers that allows for 30-year amortization on new pre-construction deals. Some people prefer a 25-year amortization, which has both advantages and disadvantages. If you're looking to borrow more or qualify for a larger mortgage, opting for a 30-year amortization makes it easier to qualify. Later in this book, I'll share some strategies to mitigate the extra interest costs that come with a longer amortization.

Having covered amortization, let's move on to the term. In Canada, terms range from 6-month convertible to 1, 2, 3, 4, 5, 6, 7, up to 10-year fixed terms, as well as 3 and 5-year variable terms. Those who opted for variable terms in 2020 are still struggling in 2024, largely due to government policies. The variable rate is tied to the prime rate, which was 2.45% and has since climbed to 8%. Many people lost substantial amounts of money, and it's unclear where that interest has gone, but it's certain it didn't stay in Canada. Most likely to support the war in Ukraine.

On the plus side, variable rates will decrease, and one of their key advantages is that breaking the mortgage incurs a smaller penalty than with a fixed term. Most "A" banks offer closed variable rates, where your monthly payment remains the same, but the proportion allocated to principal and interest changes based on the prime rate. Some lenders, like Scotia Bank and various "B" lenders, offer open variable rates, where your payments adjust every time the prime rate changes.

While it's currently harder to secure a variable rate, it will become easier once the market stabilizes, and I would recommend it for those looking to sell their investment properties soon, as the penalty for breaking a variable rate is lower. Fixed terms, on the other hand, are ideal for those who want stability and don't want to worry about market fluctuations. Many people secured 5-year fixed terms at 1.39% in 2020, but I feel for them when their mortgage renews in 2025, as their payments could rise from $2,800 to over $5,000 per month unless rates decrease—which they will.

Now is actually a good time to buy property, as many investors who purchased during the 2020 boom will likely be looking to offload their real estate. The downside of a fixed term is that breaking it carries a hefty penalty, though the bank will honor the rate, even in times of crisis. That's why it's essential to plan carefully before locking into a 5-year fixed term, especially in the current market.

Many people opt for a 3 or 5-year fixed term because they can qualify for a larger mortgage based on these rates, but not on lower or variable rates. However, keep in mind that even though fixed rates may drop, you'll continue paying the higher fixed interest rate, leading to potential losses.

Buying property with parents has become increasingly common among middle-class families. Often, young adults cannot afford to purchase a property on their own, not due to poor credit or low income, but because of the high property prices. As a result, parents frequently step in to assist their children with obtaining a mortgage. In this scenario, parents often hold a portion of the equity in the property, effectively acting like a holding corporation. If your spouse or partner defaults, the parents' equity in the property helps mitigate the risk.

There are strategies you can use, which will be discussed later in this book. However, it's important to note that if parents decide to sell their share or if they move, they will retain ownership of their portion of the property, and you would be responsible for paying land transfer tax on that share.

My advice is to purchase the property under a holding corporation if there are more than two people involved and if you do not plan to sell the property in the near future. If selling is a possibility, ensure that both you and your parents have completed your tax filings at the property's address to avoid capital gains tax from the CRA, as they may view the property as an investment. You must live at the property with your parents to avoid these taxes. If this is not feasible, either you or your parents may incur additional tax liabilities. This is a complex issue that I will address more comprehensively in a future book.

In summary, while parents' involvement can enhance your ability to buy property and offer protection, it is crucial to manage the legal and tax implications carefully. For more detailed guidance, refer to Chapter 12. And if you suspect your partner might be reading this book, I hope they aren't too concerned!

The process of purchasing a property is generally straightforward, though it may not always be quick. Once you have your income, down payment, and credit score in order, the next steps are as follows:

- **Pre-Approval**: Start by visiting a mortgage specialist to apply for a mortgage. This process typically takes 1 to 2 weeks, so be patient and don't rush. It might be fast.
- **Property Search**: After receiving mortgage approval for a specific amount, reach out to your real estate agent to begin searching for your ideal property.
- **Making an Offer**: Once you find a property you wish to buy, make an offer and provide an initial deposit.
- **Finalizing the Mortgage**: Return to your mortgage specialist to finalize the mortgage details.
- **Pre-Approval Duration**: Keep in mind that some banks may hold your pre-approval for up to 3 months, while others might extend it to a year, depending on the specialist.
- **Closing the Deal**: Once the mortgage is finalized, you will meet with the bank to review and sign all mortgage documents.
- **Legal Documentation**: Instructions are then sent to the lawyer, who will handle the signing of documents with the borrowers and provide the final bill detailing the amount owed and payment instructions.
- **Final Steps**: The borrowers will bring a cheque to finalize the transaction. Once completed, the lawyer will provide the keys to the property, and you can move in.

There are many behind-the-scenes activities involved in this process, which I will cover in more detail in my next book.

<u>Fees to Anticipate When Buying a Property</u>

One of the most common surprises for buyers are the various fees associated with purchasing a property. Many people are caught off guard by these costs because they were not properly informed beforehand. As a responsible mortgage specialist, it is crucial to explain these fees to clients, rather than relying on real estate agents, who might not always provide a complete picture.

Here is a breakdown of the fees you should expect:

- **Initial Deposit**: When placing an offer, you will need to provide an initial deposit. This amount is specific to the offer and location, such as in Ontario. Can range from $5,000 and up to $100,000.
- **Down Payment**: You will need to show the bank that you have the necessary funds for the down payment once your offer is accepted and your mortgage is approved.
- **Appraisal Fees**: Banks typically charge around $300 for appraisal fees, though this can sometimes be waived depending on the mortgage specialist. So be nice to the specialist.
- **Legal Fees**: The lawyer handling your purchase will charge a fee, which usually ranges from $1,500 to $3,000.
- **Land Transfer Tax**: This tax, payable to the government, varies by location and province. It can range from $5,000 to $20,000, depending on the property's purchase value.
- **Additional Fees for New Builds**: If you are buying a pre-construction property from a builder, additional fees such as builder fees and HST tax may apply, especially if you plan to rent the property out.
- **Energy and Gas Security Deposits**: When setting up your utility accounts, you will need to pay security deposits to the energy and gas companies.
- **Moving Costs**: Don't forget to budget for moving expenses and any repair costs for the property.

It's important to be aware of these fees in advance to avoid unexpected financial stress. Many buyers are startled by the additional costs beyond the initial deposit and down payment, often leading them to scramble for funds or resort to credit cards. In some cases, particularly with builder deals, these unexpected expenses can jeopardize the transaction.

Being prepared for these fees can help ensure a smoother buying process and prevent last-minute issues.

The Role of Personal Character in Mortgage Approval

One often-overlooked criterion in the mortgage approval process is personal character. This may seem unusual, but after a decade of working with clients, patterns emerge that suggest personal traits can influence financial outcomes.

Personal Character and Mortgage Approval:

- **Impact on Approval**: It may sound unconventional, but in some cases, individuals with a less favorable disposition may find it difficult to secure a mortgage, regardless of their credit score and income. This is not to suggest a direct causation, but there appears to be an intangible factor at play that affects the approval process.

- **Good People**: Even individuals with excellent credit and income can face challenges in obtaining a mortgage. Sometimes, this may be due to a deeper, perhaps intuitive sense that proceeding with the purchase might not be in their best interest. If you find yourself in this situation, try not to get discouraged. It could be a sign to pause and reassess. Trust that a favorable opportunity will present itself in due time.

- **Improving Personal Traits**: For those who feel they may be facing obstacles due to personal characteristics, it's worth investing time in self-improvement. Positive changes in behavior and attitude can lead to better financial outcomes and opportunities. Just as in physics, where actions and reactions follow certain principles, personal growth can lead to improved circumstances.

Understanding that personal character may play a role in the approval process can provide a different perspective. If you face obstacles, use this insight to guide your journey and work towards personal and financial growth.

CHAPTER 2: BRIDGE LOAN AND WHEN TO SET CLOSING DATE

I have a complicated relationship with bridge loans: I love them as an individual, but I find them challenging as a broker.

For a single person, moving on short notice is relatively straightforward, and you typically don't need a bridge loan. However, once you're married and have to manage logistics for a family, having the option of a bridge loan becomes crucial. Why?

Imagine you've sold your house on July 30th but have already bought a new property that's set to be yours on July 15th. You don't have the funds to pay the new property's seller yet because the sale of your current home hasn't gone through. In this case, a bank can provide a bridge loan to cover the interim period of the down payment.

Bridge loans come with high interest rates, usually prime rate plus 2%, and are charged daily. For example, if you need a bridge loan of $20,000 for 15 days, the daily interest would be calculated as follows:

$20,000 x 8% = $1,600
$1,600 / 365 days = $4.38 per day
$4.38 x 15 days = $65.70

While $65.70 for 15 days might not seem excessive, the costs can escalate if you need $250,000 for 30 days. Additionally, banks are cautious about issuing bridge loans, especially if you have lines of credit, as they might assume you'll use these credit lines instead.

Securing bridge loans can be difficult for mortgage specialists because of the risks involved. Banks are wary of extending bridge loans for extended periods due to the lack of security. If the buyer of your property fails to secure final mortgage approval and the bridge loan extends beyond the original term, a lawyer might require the buyer to cover the per diem charge. Bridge loans can typically be extended for up to six months, but if the situation fails, it can lead to significant complications.

Lawyers often dislike handling bridge loans due to the extra work and potential for ongoing issues, which can lead to additional charges for clients.

When setting the closing date, I highly recommend avoiding the end of the month, especially if it falls on a Friday. If any issues arise and we're unable to close on time, we're left in limbo for two days with limited options for resolution, leading to unnecessary stress over the weekend.

For a smoother process, aim to schedule the closing date in the middle of the month and in the middle of the week. This timing provides a buffer of business days to address any potential problems that may arise. This way, if something does go wrong, there are a few days available to resolve it before the weekend.

The beginning and end of the month can be particularly hectic, akin to Boxing Day, with response times from central offices stretching from hours to days. Errors or delays can take significantly longer to address because of the high volume of transactions and the added pressure on the rush department.

Additionally, the funding department might not release the funds on time, potentially causing issues with the deal, such as the sellers exiting the transaction or suing for the delay. While this is not common, it can happen.

To avoid these complications, ensure that your real estate agent schedules the closing date for the middle of the month. Trust me, it will make the process much smoother and less stressful.

CHAPTER 3: OLD FOLKS AND MORTGAGES

I have two key points to share with the older generation, especially those approaching retirement. First, if you're nearing retirement, consider taking out as many loans as possible before you retire. Once you've retired, securing loans becomes much more difficult.

You might be thinking, "I don't need loans" or that adding financial pressure isn't necessary. But trust me, after working hard all your life, if you only have one property and an RRSP account with no kids, you may find it challenging to fully enjoy your pension. I'm not trying to discourage you, but with the way the government is handling things, the financial situation is likely to become more difficult over time.

The Canadian population is aging more quickly than anticipated, and soon, many seniors will be relying on the next generation for support. Unfortunately, the current government has done little to prevent further economic strain, leaving the older generation dependent on government assistance.

Instead of borrowing money to cover expenses, the government should focus on building factories and leveraging Canada's resources to become more competitive in the market.

Once you retire, banks often view you as unemployed and a high-risk borrower, questioning how you'll manage monthly loan payments, especially if your credit is maxed out. This is particularly true for many retirees who have minimal investments or RRSP savings. Most rely solely on government pensions, and only a limited number receive additional employer pensions.

Given these changes in income, banks take notice. Before retiring, it's essential to ensure you're financially prepared. We'll explore various scenarios to help you assess your financial standing and find ways to improve it.

If you're someone like John Smith, approaching 65 in a few months, with a family, some savings, and a primary residence, your financial situation might look stable. You've paid off most of your mortgage, but still have a few more years left to go.

If I were in your position, I would consider remortgaging or getting a secured line of credit for the maximum loan-to-value that the bank allows. Interest rates fluctuate with different economic cycles, so depending on the current rates, it's smart to take those extra funds and diversify your investments.

For example, if you can reborrow $250K, I'd split it into three streams. First, consider private lending. If you're unfamiliar with mortgages and private loans, I recommend looking into a Mortgage Investment Corporation (MIC). Be sure to verify that it's registered, as there are fraudulent companies out there. The difference is typically a 12-14% return with private lending vs. an 8-9% return with an MIC. For beginners, I'd suggest going with an MIC. You could allocate $100K here, expecting around $1K in monthly returns.

For the remaining $150K, I'd invest in pre-construction condos, keeping a few things in mind. Avoid buying in the hottest markets and ensure the property comes with an assignment option. Since you're retiring soon, once the builder completes the condo, your income might not be sufficient to get mortgage approval. Most banks won't approve you unless you've secured financing in advance, which can be done up to four years before completion.

The assignment option allows you to resell the project to a third party at a higher price if demand increases. This way, you not only recoup your initial deposit but also potentially earn extra profit without having to secure a mortgage or find tenants. However, be mindful that property values might not rise as expected. If that happens, you may need to close the property and take on a mortgage.

If you're still working, apply for the mortgage on the pre-construction project now, increasing your chances of keeping the property and selling it off when the market is in demand. Not all banks offer pre-construction mortgages, and some have options up to four years. Choose carefully, especially if you're close to retirement and your income will change once the project is completed.

I'm sure many people will wonder, "Why invest in pre-construction when you could buy a duplex and rent it out?" That's also a great idea, but if you've never dealt with tenants or if you're purchasing at a high interest rate, think twice.

There are a few important factors to consider before buying a rental property. Do you have at least six months' worth of expenses saved after covering the closing costs? These closing costs include the down payment, legal fees, and government taxes. If you have several months' worth of expenses set aside, that's fantastic. It means you won't be pulling your hair out if issues arise—and believe me, I'm serious about that!

Next, let's look at the current mortgage rates. If they're below or close to 3%, that's a rate we can work with. However, if the property's value exceeds $1 million, it's a different story. With a small down payment, your cash flow will be negative, and you'll have to cover the shortfall out of pocket for a long time. So, factors like mortgage rates, current market value, and potential rental income must be carefully considered before buying a rental property.

If you're in your 60s and it's just you and your spouse, don't add unnecessary stress to your life. Stick to the initial, less complicated investment pathway.

If you have less than $250K after reborrowing, say around $50K, and you're living in Toronto, it's best to rethink your strategy. The most practical approach might be private lending, but exercise caution—never lend more than 75% of the appraised value. Alternatively, consider Mortgage Investment Corporations (MICs) instead of GICs or Mutual Funds. While those traditional products can generate income, they typically don't do so quickly and are highly dependent on the stock market. Again, this is not financial advice!

What if you're someone like John Smith, but with a long way to go in paying off your mortgage and a lot of outstanding loans? Well, my friend, you're not alone. You're similar to many of my clients whom I expect to see in the next 10 to 20 years.

The issue in Toronto is that people have shifted their needs and wants, turning housing into a speculative commodity. While having a roof over one's head is a basic necessity, many in Toronto view real estate as an investment that continuously appreciates, leading to heavy speculation. If this speculation could be curbed, everyone might be able to enjoy living in the city. However, capitalism, along with location and other factors, makes this unlikely.

The government failed to foresee this and didn't develop a 10- to 25-year plan for the city. Since 2016, the landscape has changed drastically, making it increasingly difficult for people to own homes. The main problem is that the government didn't establish sufficient protections for citizens; instead, they focused on the financial gains.

If you're approaching retirement with a significant amount of loans and only your primary residence, I recommend considering the following, though it's a bit of an unconventional plan. Sell your primary residence and invest the proceeds into pre-construction projects and private lending opportunities. Then, leave the country for six months, as required by the government, and relocate to places like Georgia or the Caribbean. The monthly interest you'll earn from private lending should be enough to sustain a comfortable lifestyle. Once the pre-construction project is completed, you can sell it and reinvest the lump sum. At that point, you can fully retire and focus on enjoying your life.

If you own only one house, it's important to schedule a meeting with your local mortgage specialist. Don't assume that your RRSP or investments will last throughout your retirement. While having these assets is beneficial, I've observed that they can be depleted due to unforeseen life events, which often leads the older generation to rely more heavily on them.

Another excellent strategy while you're still working is to create a holding corporation with your children. This allows you to manage the investment properties with your grown-up kids while you're still active. When you retire, you'll continue to own these properties, but you can transfer them to your children smoothly. One major issue that arises when children inherit multiple investment properties is dealing with mortgage assumptions and capital gains taxes if they decide to sell.

If you establish a holding corporation and purchase an investment property through it, you can transfer these properties to your children without requiring them to remortgage. Although not all major banks offer this option, it significantly eases the process for your children, as they won't need to apply for new mortgages after your passing. When you die, the bank will eventually discover this and may ask your children if they can financially support the property. If they cannot, they might need to sell it and pay capital gains tax if the property is deemed an investment by the CRA, due to its non-residential status.

While there are numerous benefits to having a holding corporation, one major drawback is the double taxation: you pay taxes when you purchase and again when you sell based on the market value. Having more children can be financially advantageous in the long run, provided they are properly educated. Family unity and shared values can be a strong financial asset.

If you are renting and do not own any property, you are not alone, and it can be challenging to improve your financial situation under these circumstances. With house speculation being unpredictable, it's crucial to save as much as possible. Consider aiming to buy a property with a 5% down payment, such as a pre-construction home. This can be advantageous as the property's value increases during construction, and some builders offer options for monthly payments instead of a lump sum.

Be cautious if you choose to stop making rental payments to save for a down payment, as this can lead to complications. Alternatively, you might explore borrowing against your RRSP to invest in mutual funds or other assets. This strategy can be challenging, especially if you lack long-term support from family or are managing on your own, but it's not impossible.

Many creative strategies can help generate additional cash flow. Seek a financial advisor who will take the time to review your situation and provide tailored advice. Additionally, consider establishing a sole proprietorship or corporation, which could open opportunities for business loans. While this path can be complex, it offers potential avenues for financial growth. More details will be covered in the next financial book.

CHAPTER 4: YOUNG GENERATION THAT IS SCREWED OR 5% DOWN PAYMENT NATION

It's going to be hard, but it's possible. Things won't get easier, but I'll outline a few pathways that can help you work towards owning your first residence. Some might ask, "Why own a property when you can rent or invest elsewhere?" Trust me, the goal isn't to push you into a big loan or earn a commission. Yes, homeownership means taking on the largest loan of your life, but with the right understanding, you can break the cycle of housing insecurity.

Homeowners tend to be happier and more financially secure than renters. Of course, you can make mistakes—investing in the wrong property or buying at the wrong time can bring challenges and stress. That's why it's essential to sit down and carefully review your numbers to determine if now is the right time for you. Yes, it's financially challenging, but if you purchase the right property at the right time, the return on investment can exceed regular financial products.

Plus, in a place like Ontario, where properties are surrounded by the Great Lakes, your investment is tied to one of the world's most valuable future resources: fresh water. If inflation rises sharply again, your money is safer in property, especially in a region where living may become increasingly coveted in the future.

Since 2016, the government introduced a stress test for both types of homebuyers—those putting down less than 20% and needing insurance, and those putting down more than 20%. This is where the challenges began, creating a significant hurdle for future generations. As you accumulate loans while growing up, securing a mortgage becomes increasingly difficult, with banks likely to decline your application.

Here's a fun fact that might surprise many of you: The USSR didn't have a mortgage system. People had the right to choose where they would live. For example, my mother, who was a veterinarian, chose her place of work about twenty minutes from the main city. She and my father were given a semi-detached house, and it was under their ownership or title. They only needed to cover utility costs.

If someone wanted to move to the city, it was a lengthy process but still possible, taking about 3-4 months—similar to the time it takes to sell property and move here. While you wouldn't get a penthouse, most people didn't chase after luxury. They were content. Those who worked hard could aim for higher-end housing, but there wasn't a widespread desire for excess.

In capitalism, people often speculate, manipulate the market, and rely heavily on real estate brokers. And let's not forget the bank, which might not even approve your mortgage. While there's freedom in choosing a property and setting your price in a capitalist system, imagine not needing a mortgage at all—no down payment, no loan. In the USSR, the government would give you property for free when you were ready to move out from your parents' home.

Achieving something like this in our society would take time and considerable effort from the government, but it's not impossible.

Perhaps within 20 years, we could see a change.

So, fellow Canadians, we're out of luck. We might have to wait another three hundred years before communism comes to Canada, but until then, it's time to start saving for that down payment. Here are some simple pathways to explore different scenarios.

My personal advice: instead of spending your extra hard-earned money, begin setting aside $50-$300 per month into a savings account. You'll be surprised how quickly it grows. If you have a large family, consider starting a monthly contribution from each family member to build a family trust fund. This will not only help you save, but it will also generate interest on the money you've pooled together.

There are four key things you need: a stable income, a down payment, a strong credit history, and a low loan balance.

- **Stable Income:** The higher your income, the larger the mortgage you'll qualify for, or you may need a lower down payment. Consider exploring new career opportunities as you grow to improve your income.

- **Down Payment:** Start saving and investing those funds to earn interest. While this can help your money grow, be mindful that if the market crashes, you could lose some of it. The larger your down payment, the more purchasing power you'll have. While it's difficult to save the full 20% down to avoid insurance, aim to set aside at least $25,000 for a bank down payment and an additional $5,000 to $8,000 for closing costs.

- **Credit History**: Avoid maxing out your credit cards and keep your balance below 80% of your credit limit, as this affects your credit score. If your score falls below

600, forget about applying for a mortgage—insurance companies won't review files with scores that low. If your score is between 600 and 700 (common for younger generations), it's tighter but still possible to get approved. Keep your loans manageable, and having multiple loans with no balance looks better. Watch out for annual fees as they can also hurt your credit score.

For the young generation just accepted into university and who accidentally picked up this book—you're already ahead of the game by foreseeing this situation. Start putting money aside now and ask your family to contribute to your investment account. However, don't sacrifice your education for income or a down payment. Instead, use your TFSA and make regular monthly contributions.

Keep in mind that banks won't review your mortgage application without income, a down payment, or a strong credit history. The goal is to have at least 5–10% saved up by the time you graduate for your down payment and closing costs. Note that closing costs are in addition to the down payment. For example, if you purchase a $500K property with a 5% down payment ($25,000), closing costs—including lawyer fees, utility setup, land transfer taxes, and other possible expenses—could add up to an additional $10K.

There are a couple of paths you can take, though they carry risks if you don't want to wait until you graduate. If you're in university, consider starting a holding corporation and inviting people—preferably family members—to join in on buying a property. However, the more shareholders involved, the riskier and more complicated it becomes, so carefully choose the right partners. If you purchase under a holding corporation, it will require a 20% down payment to avoid insurance.

Alternatively, use your TFSA or family contributions to invest. Ask your parents or older relatives to help find a good pre-construction project from a reliable builder. Some projects allow a 5% down payment with monthly installments or lump sums. It's also beneficial if the builder allows you to assign the property to a third party for a higher price before you even need to get a mortgage. Keep in mind, though, that builders usually require pre-approval before committing to a sale.

In the end, it's all about choosing people you trust and can rely on—family is often the best place to start your real estate journey. If you have strong friends, sit them down and explain the potential risks and rewards. For some, it's better to invest extra money into something that could generate significant returns rather than spending it on things that won't matter in the long run.

For the young generation that just graduated from university or college and stumbled upon this book—there's a chance for a brighter future, but it's going to be a long road.

First, focus on finding a job and positioning yourself for higher pay as your experience grows. Once your income is stable, start putting away at least 10–20% of it each month toward your down payment. Consider using a TFSA connected to low-fee ETFs to help grow your savings over time, though be aware you could lose money if the market turns.

One of the challenges many young graduates face is accumulating a significant amount of debt, often due to student loans. This is largely a result of government policies that have burdened young people with debt as soon as they enter the workforce. So, is it worth paying off these loans before applying for a mortgage? From the banks' and insurance companies' perspectives, yes, but from an investor's viewpoint, the focus should be on building wealth rather than simply paying off creditors.If you lived in the USSR, there was no student debt, and you didn't have to worry about a down payment.

Another common issue for younger generations is managing their credit. The more debt you carry, the harder it becomes to get approved for a mortgage, especially since the introduction of the government's stress test after 2016. This stress test was implemented to prevent a mortgage collapse and cool down the first-time homebuyer market, but it has made it harder for young people to afford a home. While the intent was to protect the market, many believe there could have been better ways to address the issue.

The fewer loans you have, the higher your chances of being approved for a larger mortgage, as your file will be reviewed under a 25-year amortization period, as required by insurance. Your file is evaluated by two parties: first by the bank and then by the insurance company. The reason insurance is involved is straightforward and represents what I call "perfect capitalism." They secure the bank by providing three months of payments before the bank can take away your property. The interesting part is that the premium you pay towards the insurance, which is added to your mortgage, essentially covers those three months of payments in case you default. Plus, they add extra to account for their risk. While this does offer some protection to the borrower and insurance companies do assume risk, the system could be simpler, and we could create a better environment for everyone. Unfortunately, such ideas won't be accepted, and future generations will continue to face these challenges.

Once you've secured a stable income, built up your down payment, and maintained low loan balances, you'll reach the milestone of turning thirty. At this point, it's essential to set your priorities. If buying a property is on your agenda, be prepared to make sacrifices along the way. It would be ideal if the government provided a free home upon securing a job, but such a system is unlikely in a capitalist society. However, it was a reality in the USSR.

For young adults who have graduated from university or college, are currently working, and are either renting or living with their parents: if you're renting, it's a good start, but are you saving for a down payment? If not, consider moving back in with your parents temporarily to save a substantial amount of money instead of paying someone else's mortgage.

Some argue that owning property is a fixed asset that can't be liquidated quickly, which may pose challenges in the long run. While owning a property and managing a mortgage can be burdensome, if you plan to stay in one place and eventually pass the property on to your children, it could be a more advantageous option.

By staying with your parents, you can save up for a down payment and afford a property you truly want, rather than settling for what you can currently afford. Instead of letting your savings accumulate in a regular account, consider investing 100% of those savings into ETFs connected to a TFSA account, which offers tax-free interest earnings. Although investing in ETFs carries risk, choosing ones with dividends could be profitable in the long run. It's crucial to find a competent financial planner, but also conduct your own research to ensure your money is managed wisely.

If you're renting and have no alternative housing, start saving diligently. A cautionary tale from one of my clients involved them stopping rent payments to save for a down payment. Don't neglect your obligations to your landlord—communicate with them because, ultimately, karma has a way of catching up.

For medical residents and doctors dealing with the challenges of the OHIP system and looking to buy a home: you're in a favorable position. Start by saving up at least 5 to 10 percent for a down payment and purchase a property. If your residency or internship lasts around 5 years, why pay rent when you could own a property? Once your practice is complete, you can recover your down payment and potentially earn a profit when you sell the property at the right time.

Banks often consider your future income, so as long as you have the down payment, you may find it easier to get approved. If I were in your position, I would form a coalition with fellow residents to buy an investment property that could generate rental income and appreciate over time.

Note that some banks may apply this rule of assumed future income for up to 2 years after your residency, so make sure to leverage this opportunity. However, be aware that if you plan to open your own medical practice, having an investment property might impact your credibility, as it could be seen as a liability. Balancing mortgage payments and your credit is crucial to maintaining financial stability in both areas.

Before 2016, it was considerably easier for first-time buyers to purchase a property. Many young individuals bought condominium units and grew their investments as they progressed. In my opinion, one reason the government might have avoided assisting the younger generation with property ownership could be the ease of controlling people who don't own assets. Beyond economic factors like price growth and limited housing inventory, renting means you are paying someone else's mortgage and don't own your property. This creates mental pressure and limits your comfort and freedom in a rental unit.

On the other hand, when you own property—or more accurately, when the bank owns it and you are maintaining it—it becomes harder for the government to exert control over you. The central bank of Canada significantly raised interest rates from 2022 to 2023. Given this, it's not unreasonable to be concerned about potential increases in rental rates as well. If you're facing difficulties, it might be time to demand housing reform.

CHAPTER 5: BANK LOOPHOLES

There are many loopholes in the banking system, but discussing them here would breach professional ethics. Additionally, even with this knowledge, there's limited action you can take since it's ultimately up to the mortgage specialist to decide what's reasonable.

For instance, if you purchase a property through a holding corporation, it won't appear on your credit report. This allows you to acquire additional properties through other holding corporations without impacting your credit profile. This approach can help you avoid higher interest rates typically associated with commercial banking. However, if a mortgage specialist fails to perform due diligence and disclose information about holding properties, the responsibility falls on them.

If you need to get a car, it's better to finance it rather than lease it. Financing allows you to own the asset and often provides similar tax savings as leasing. Additionally, consider purchasing the car through your company, as some lenders permit the payments to be deducted from the business account. This approach can be advantageous because it keeps the loan payments off your personal financial ratios, even though they might be high. By having the payments made from the business account, it won't impact your personal ratios.

How can you make a higher income? That's a question many of us ask daily. Sometimes, your current income isn't enough to support a purchase or refinance, so you'll need to either increase your down payment or boost your income. The bank will typically consider either a second full-time salary or business income. When it comes to business income, though, you'll need to show proof from the past two years, and let's face it, no one can predict that far ahead. So, you might need to secure a second job for the time being and use that income when applying for refinancing or purchasing.

It may seem impossible, but think of the difference between paying 7% or 3% in interest. That's a significant gap when you look at the amortization schedule and see how much interest you're potentially losing. At this point, some borrowers might think, "Maybe I should find one of those creative mortgage specialists to help." Sure, it sounds like a good idea, but it's not always worth the risk and future consequences. Instead, consult with your mortgage specialist to determine how much extra income you'll need to qualify for the amount you're seeking.

Again, there are many loopholes related to income, but I can't disclose all of them. Sharing this information could lead to their widespread use, prompting banks to tighten their programs. This could ultimately shut down mortgage sales channels and shift the industry towards virtual approvals, which have a lower success rate.

For credit scores, if you're faced with the choice between saving for a down payment or paying off credit debt, most experienced mortgage specialists would advise focusing on the down payment. To maintain a high or good credit score, keep your credit utilization below 80% of your credit limits. Make timely payments and keep multiple credit lines open, as this lowers your overall utilization if you don't max out all your credit cards. Avoid maxing out your credit lines, as this will negatively impact your credit score.

Maintain a balance below 80% on your credit cards and ensure regular monthly payments to build a positive payment history. Be cautious with telecom companies, as they may report unpaid bills to collections, which can significantly harm your credit score.

If you've recently paid off your credit cards and your mortgage specialist needs to pull your credit report, ask them to wait and request an update from Equifax. Provide proof of your payments with the request. This can expedite the update process, potentially improving your credit score in 2 to 4 weeks, rather than waiting the usual 3 months. Even a 5-point increase in your credit score can significantly affect your approval chances.

For instance, with a beacon score of 680 or higher, your Gross Debt Service (GDS) and Total Debt Service (TDS) ratios might be 39% and 44%, respectively. If your score is lower, the ratios might be 36% and 42%. GDS calculates your mortgage payment, property taxes, and heating costs as a percentage of your income, while TDS includes your credit line payments as well.

CHAPTER 6: HOW MORTGAGE SPECIALISTS SCREW YOU ;)

This aspect of our job is quite intriguing. Beyond the routine of waking up, enjoying a coffee, and driving your Porsche to the office, there are three types of mortgage specialists we'll discuss in this chapter. Let's start with my least favorite: "The All-Clients-Are-Whores" specialist.

These mortgage specialists show little genuine concern for your well-being, although they may give the impression that they do. They might promise to secure a mortgage for you at exorbitant rates, such as 15% interest plus a 3% lender fee, making the total interest rate 18%. I encountered many of these specialists before the SARS-CoV-2 pandemic and its aftermath. I anticipate that a new generation of such practitioners may emerge as the industry evolves.

Why do some mortgage specialists view all clients as mere "interest seekers"? These brokers are primarily focused on making money and maintaining a favorable image. They know clients come to them because they face limited options, so they adopt a seemingly accommodating approach. However, if you agree to their terms immediately, they might offer a more pleasant experience.

The trouble begins when clients start to question or negotiate, often weeks before closing. This is where many people make mistakes by leaving crucial tasks until the last minute, giving these brokers the opportunity to take advantage. Rather than offering competitive rates, they may propose the highest possible interest rates. Instead of providing cashbacks, they might charge exorbitant fees, sometimes up to 10% of the loan amount.

My advice is to consult with an adviser and seek a second opinion. It's crucial not to rush into decisions, as this can lead to costly mistakes. A common pitfall is when mortgage brokers promise approval for an amount far beyond your income—such as $1M with just a $5K annual income—while offering seemingly attractive rates like 2%. Some clients accept these terms, only to face issues later on. Brokers who focus solely on profit may secure a deal for themselves but provide poor service if complications arise. For example, out of 10 clients, if 5 get approved with a $750K mortgage, the broker earns roughly $37K in net profit. However, if the deal falls through, these brokers may become unresponsive and blame the client. Consequently, clients may discover that major banks have flagged their profiles, resulting in a credit score drop below 600 points.

Identifying a reliable mortgage specialist is not as difficult as it may seem. Focus on two key factors: their communication style and their demeanor. A professional specialist will maintain simplicity and avoid flaunting their success, as they are not driven by greed. Some might question why a specialist drives a luxury car like a Porsche, but often, the monthly payments are comparable to more modest vehicles like a Honda Accord, and insurance costs are lower for various reasons.

When you meet with a mortgage specialist, observe the environment. A well-appointed office can be impressive, but a simpler, more approachable setting is often preferable. If the office seems ostentatious, be prepared for potentially inflated fees.

Pay close attention to how the specialist communicates. A good specialist will guide you through the process transparently, while a less reputable one might make you feel comfortable but leave you with lingering concerns.

The key is that a reputable specialist will present you with various options and respect your decisions, rather than pressuring you into uncomfortable agreements. Always ensure that you address important matters early in the process to avoid unexpected costs later.

The second type of mortgage specialist is the "wannabe" specialist. They may seem uninterested in your mortgage because they either have other priorities or lack the expertise needed to handle your mortgage properly. Identifying them can be challenging, especially in today's fast-paced world where everyone seems busy, partly due to government inefficiencies.

These specialists might have good intentions and genuinely want you to achieve your goals, but their lack of dedication can lead to issues. I learned this the hard way by spending countless hours on the phone over several months to ensure a file was properly set up and funded. Many specialists, however, handle files casually, which can result in mistakes and even declined applications due to inadequate attention to detail.

To avoid these pitfalls, it's best to steer clear of specialists who don't demonstrate thoroughness and commitment.

I faced challenges when I was first hired by the bank, with no one to guide me through the complexities of the mortgage industry. I had to navigate and learn on my own. Each file I handled required 2 to 3 hours of preparation to ensure it was ready for submission. Now, I can manage the same tasks in less than 30 minutes—unless dealing with clients who own multiple properties, which I find particularly interesting. Over time, I've gained enough knowledge to act as a resource for both newly hired and experienced mortgage specialists. Ironically, I still provide guidance to seasoned professionals and vice versa, as I occasionally miss meetings about new programs. This situation arose because the training I received, despite being extensive, was insufficient. One of the reasons banks struggle with profitability is the lack of effective training and the presence of poor educational resources.

Whatever new knowledge specialists acquire, I often find myself reteaching it in various ways to align with each underwriter's preferences. After all, we're all human, and our individual tastes—like our coffee preferences—vary.

I was nearly fired because of my unconventional thinking, but I owe a huge thanks to my manager at the time who understood and protected me. As I learned how to file deals, I was often frustrated by the lack of teaching and support. The system made me feel like just another peasant compared to their perceived status of being Zeus from Mount Olympus. This disconnect can either make or break brokers. While I understand that banks can't disclose all their loopholes, at least they could guide us to avoid common mistakes. Wannabe specialists often struggle to get deals approved and waste extra time because of this lack of proper training.

Don't confuse these specialists with those who constantly ask for additional documents; it's normal for underwriters to request more information as they review the file. For example, in December 2019, just one week before closing, we had to make minor changes to an almost complete file because the underwriter requested additional proof of ongoing income. While it makes sense for the bank to follow up on borrower income, it can be frustrating when changes are requested after approval. Specialists should always inform clients of potential risks associated with making changes and be aware that clients might sue if these risks are not communicated.

Lastly, the mortgage specialists you want to work with are those who aren't just chasing after the smallest rate difference, like 0.05%. These dedicated professionals are the ones who work tirelessly, often staying up all night to get things done. While they may accept small tokens of appreciation from clients, their main goal is to build a genuine professional relationship, not just a transactional interaction.

These specialists aim to create a robust professional network that benefits both them and their clients. They are not seeking a fleeting one-time deal but rather a lasting relationship, akin to a marriage, where they go the extra mile to ensure you get the best possible outcome. Their objective is not to charge exorbitant rates or fees but to provide valuable support and service, which can lead to repeat business and referrals.

Good mortgage specialists tend to focus on doing their job well because they are well-compensated by the banks. Finding these rare professionals who prioritize building lasting relationships over short-term gains can be challenging, but they are worth the effort. They usually say " I just press buttons " .

CHAPTER 7: SKIP OTHER CHAPTERS IF YOU NEED TO GET A MORTGAGE, GUIDE TO SUCCESS

This is my favorite chapter, and this is why you invested in this book.

If you're a Canadian currently renting and relying solely on pension for retirement, it's time to make a change. Start setting aside money for a down payment—just $300 a month can make a difference. Alternatively, you can team up with family members to pool resources and combine incomes towards a mortgage. The power of numbers means that the more people involved, the higher your chances of success. If family isn't an option, consider asking friends or coworkers to join forces and start a holding corporation. Each participant contributes their income and savings towards the purchase.

Look for a property in the Greater Toronto Area or another major city. Ideally, a duplex or fourplex that you can rent out. While managing rental properties can be challenging and initially low in returns, the long-term benefits can be substantial. When you eventually sell, the profits can be significant.

Diversify your investment portfolio with various assets such as ETFs, private lending, and precious metals like silver. Additionally, consider getting universal life insurance for long-term protection, and term life insurance for short-term needs. Term life insurance is cheaper and provides essential coverage for unexpected life events, though it doesn't accumulate cash value. Universal life insurance, while more expensive, offers investment opportunities and allows you to withdraw money tax-free. Unlike RRSPs, which require taxes upon withdrawal, universal life insurance provides both protection and a tax-free return on investment.

For low-income families, the journey to homeownership can be challenging, but taking the first step involves building a strong support network of family and friends. Consider borrowing against your RRSP, which can be done through a bank or other financial institution. However, be aware that using an RRSP loan for a down payment has its drawbacks. The primary concern is that the monthly payments on the RRSP loan will be added to your liabilities.

It's crucial to note that if you borrow against your RRSP for the down payment from one bank, you should obtain your mortgage from the same bank. This is because the bank providing the mortgage will only use the interest payments from the RRSP loan in their calculations, which gives you some leeway. This can be beneficial, as it allows you to apply for a mortgage with a 5% down payment. Keep in mind that insurance companies are very strict with their rules and regulations, so working with the same institution for both the RRSP loan and the mortgage can help streamline the process.

When you get a mortgage, your primary goal should be to view the property as an investment, not a luxury. In the capitalist world, property is essentially a commodity: you buy it and sell it when the timing is right.

For pre-construction properties, the process is straightforward. You might purchase a property for $500K, and if the market is favorable when construction is completed, you could sell it for $700K within the next five years. This can provide a substantial passive income if you decide to sell before the property officially closes. However, be cautious and conduct thorough research, as poor location choices or market fluctuations could impact your returns.

If you're buying a resale property, consider renovating it to increase its value. Transforming a property into a duplex or adding additional units can provide extra income to help pay down your mortgage more quickly. This added value can also make the property worth more when you decide to sell. Location is critical, so analyze market trends carefully. For example, during the SARS-COV-2 lockdowns, there was a surge in cottage purchases, leading to a spike in prices. However, as the market stabilizes, some of these properties are not selling for the same prices they were bought for.

For condos, strategic purchasing and timing are essential. You need to evaluate where to buy and how long to hold onto the property before selling. For houses, focus on making strategic improvements that generate income or choosing locations that are likely to increase in value. Avoid extensive renovations that won't significantly enhance your property's value relative to the neighborhood. Even if you invest in high-end upgrades, the overall appeal of the property is closely tied to its location and the surrounding area.

I prefer to buy properties through a holding corporation, with each corporation managing a separate property. My strategy typically involves starting with a fourplex, managing it for 1-3 years, and then refinancing to extract the equity. This equity is then invested in secure options like private lending. The goal is to continue acquiring properties, such as triplexes or fourplexes, and building a substantial portfolio over time.

Buying properties through a holding corporation offers the advantage of long-term retention and generational transfer without triggering double taxation upon sale. Rental income collected through these corporations does not impact your personal income tax bracket and provides protection from the CRA. However, it's crucial to not invest all your funds solely in properties. Diversify your portfolio with investments and savings, and consider purchasing physical silver bars instead of paper assets.

If you choose a 30-year amortization, there are a few strategies to save on interest payments to the bank. First and foremost, buying property at the right time and location is crucial; ideally, the appreciation of the property will compensate for the interest paid when you eventually sell. However, this outcome is not guaranteed. It's important to prioritize saving and investing before focusing on paying creditors. To reduce interest, consider converting your monthly mortgage payments to weekly or bi-weekly accelerated payments, or simply increase your monthly payment slightly. If possible, making lump-sum payments towards the mortgage can also help in reducing the principal faster, though many banks only permit such payments after the first six months of your mortgage. Additionally, if you have extra funds, investing in stocks or other assets might be beneficial. Even though there's a risk of loss, the potential for gains can be more advantageous than paying all interest to the bank. By implementing these strategies, you can minimize the total interest paid over the life of your mortgage and enhance your overall financial returns.

You have read chapters 5 and 6 on income, which will provide you with insight into the mortgage sector. To buy a property, start by organizing your documents and ensuring you have a solid income. Visit a mortgage specialist; although many may seem knowledgeable, you'll eventually find the right one for your needs.

Once you've found a suitable specialist, obtain a pre-approval. Banks may offer paper approvals or digital print screens. With a conditional approval from the bank, review the conditions and determine what can be met. Typically, most conditions can be fulfilled, so you'll have a clear idea of what to expect from the bank. Next, work with your real estate agent to find the right property. Remember, even though you might live in the property initially and make cosmetic renovations, it is an investment, and you will eventually move out. Finalize the purchase and complete the mortgage process once you've found the right property.

If you're lacking income or a down payment, consider setting up a holding corporation and involving as many friends or family members as possible. Once you have a combined income of over $100K and savings from each participant, it can potentially work. However, be mindful of liabilities—some members may be more of a burden than a benefit, so choose carefully who joins your venture.

CHAPTER 8: FU*CK UPS

We are all human and mistakes are inevitable, so try not to be too hard on us. You'll find more interesting anecdotes in my next book, including a story about a mortgage specialist who regretted ever getting his license. It's a common experience, especially for newcomers; the first six months can be particularly challenging without a mentor.

In this chapter, I'll keep it brief, but the key takeaway is that mortgage specialists do make mistakes. To help us avoid them, remember that sending 20 separate emails with individual documents can delay your file's review. We may forget or simply not have the time to open and review each document promptly, causing procrastination. A little push can often help us stay focused and ensure your file gets the attention it needs.

Sometimes mortgage specialists input incorrect information into the file, which often causes delays in the review process. This is frequently due to errors with income data, so providing comprehensive information from the beginning helps us understand your file better. Remember, we don't always know exactly what you need.

Another common issue arises when we have to figure out the final purchase price of a property, especially if there have been significant upgrades over time. For example, if you initially purchased a property for $513,978 and, after five years of upgrades, the price has risen to $620,000, let the mortgage specialist know the final purchase price directly. This can prevent additional costs or complications with your down payment, so it's important to be precise and proactive.

One of the most frustrating aspects is the lack of communication. It's a common issue among mortgage specialists who fail to follow up. This could be attributed to excessive daily phone interactions, which might affect their responsiveness. It's particularly problematic when your file has been declined, and a mortgage specialist takes days to inform you, leaving you under the impression that everything is still progressing well. When they then fail to return your calls or answer your inquiries, it can be incredibly distressing.

If you encounter such mortgage specialists, it's advisable to seek alternatives. However, please remember that if we don't answer your call immediately or within a few hours, it's not because we are neglecting you. We often juggle multiple tasks simultaneously —answering phone lines, responding to emails, and managing team chats. Sometimes, urgent matters require our full attention, and a random customer inquiry may seem intrusive.

If you have concerns, visiting the branch in person might be a better option. Mortgage specialists strive to respond promptly and efficiently to all communications.

CHAPTER 9: FAVOR TO ASK, MORTGAGE SPECIALIST TO BORROWERS

I believe I speak on behalf of all mortgage specialists and brokers when I say this: "Please do not send a half-cut picture of your statement." It's frustrating, and surprisingly, everyone does it—even doctors!

When a mortgage specialist requests documents, please ensure they are scanned properly and attached to the email, or bring in a hard copy. This not only looks professional but also makes our work more efficient. Imagine being the client who sends a photo taken on the kitchen counter, showing your breakfast, with poor image quality. We then have to print it, ensure it's legible, and edit the edges. This simple mistake can add an extra 3 to 4 minutes of unnecessary work, potentially delaying the review of your file to a later day or even the next day.

So, if you want your mortgage specialist to begin processing your file quickly, scan your documents correctly and follow the document list we provide—**do not** send extra, unrequested documents. Providing unnecessary documents can create complications, potentially leading to a lower mortgage amount or even a declined application. If you think of additional documents that might be helpful, **ask first**—it's possible the specialist may have simply forgotten to request them.

Another challenge we face is with clients who send one email per document, resulting in 30 emails by the end of the day because they couldn't consolidate everything into one message. What do you think happens to those files? They might get reviewed over the weekend—if time allows. This approach signals to us that you don't value our time, so naturally, we'll take our time reviewing the file when we can. Don't be surprised if your file hasn't been reviewed yet under these circumstances.

We understand that some individuals, particularly from older generations, may not be as familiar with document preparation. Don't hesitate to ask us for help—we're happy to assist.

It's crucial to send only the documents we request, and equally important to ensure they can be cross-referenced to you. Here's what I mean: sometimes clients send T4s from the CRA portal or bank statements from Scotiabank. While you know these documents are yours, how are we supposed to verify that? CRA-issued T4s don't display your name, so we need the T4 from your employer, which includes your name and other identifying details. The same goes for bank statements—some Scotiabank statements, for example, show only the account number and not the client's name. To avoid this, always provide a full monthly statement or a void cheque, so we can match the account number to your name.

There are many documents involved in the mortgage process, so please be mindful when submitting them to avoid unnecessary delays. And if you're a mortgage specialist sending documents to a colleague in 20 separate emails, rest assured they're cursing you for the lack of professionalism!

Don't buy a $2 million property just because it seems like the best idea ever, especially if you're earning $25,000 per year. Yes, the home of your dreams might be out there, and your real estate agent may be urging you to buy it, partly because they stand to earn a nice commission. Here's what often happens: clients find their dream home and rush to get a mortgage, fearing they'll miss out or go to another bank. When this happens, I usually tell them to go ahead and visit that other bank.

Dear borrowers, always consult with your mortgage specialist first—not just any branch representative who sits in the office from 9 to 5, but an actual mortgage specialist or broker. Mortgage specialists focus on your pre-approval and understand your financial situation. Branch reps may not be available when you need them most, like late in the evening when you're making an offer and need urgent advice. A mortgage specialist, on the other hand, can guide you through the process and ensure you're financially prepared.

For example, with an income of $25,000 per year, you can realistically afford a mortgage of around $50,000—not $2 million. As of summer 2024, an income of $100,000 would qualify you for a mortgage of about $500,000, and an income of $200,000 might get you closer to $1 million. Before the rate hikes, someone earning $100,000 could secure a $1 million mortgage. Hopefully, as rates decrease in the future, affordability will improve again.

What documents do you need to bring, and how do we review them?

Keep in mind that every bank has its own unique requirements, so the documents requested may vary slightly. However, to give you a rough idea, here's what we typically ask for. Also, be aware that your specialist may request additional documents throughout the process. Don't be upset—it's actually a good sign that the bank is asking for more information, as they are working to resolve any issues. So, be kind to your specialist; they are on your side.

If you are employed, the basic documents required usually include:
- Letter of employment

- T4
- Recent pay stubs
- Bank statements

If you are self-employed, the following documents will typically be needed:
- T1 General and Notice of Assessment (NOA) for the last two years
- Business registration
- Financial statements, if you have a corporation

If you own a property, you'll also need to provide:
- Property tax bill
- Mortgage statement
- Condominium fee details, if applicable, bank statement with your name

If you rent out your property, we'll need:
- Lease agreement
- Bank statements showing rental deposit transactions

For down payment verification, we usually ask for either:
- Three months of bank statements, or
- Two quarterly reports

Don't worry—some banks don't require the funds to have been sitting in a single account for three months. We just need to understand where the funds came from and how they were accumulated.

What documents do you need to buy an investment property?

The process is straightforward. You'll need the purchase agreement and the MLS listing (agent version). The purchase agreement will be provided by your agent once your offer is accepted, and the MLS listing is also supplied by the agent. The MLS listing is important as it provides key details about the property, such as property taxes, age, and other relevant information—so please don't forget to include it.

If you're purchasing an investment property from a builder, we will need the fully signed purchase agreement from the builder. **Please do not send us an unsigned copy**. Along with that, you'll need to provide a copy of the cheques or the statement of adjustments(lawyer). The statement of adjustments is typically issued by your lawyer, who represents you during the purchase, and is provided in the later stages of the transaction.

Our favorite clients are those who constantly push us, creating unnecessary pressure, and then, once the deal is completed, smile and go to another bank for a 0.05% rate difference. It's frustrating —it shows a lack of respect for both yourself and the people working hard on your behalf. These clients often argue that "it's just business" and that we should offer a better rate.

However, we choose discounts based on our discretion, and once a file is complete, we may charge slightly higher. If the file is straightforward or for a loyal, returning customer, we might go the extra mile, but you have to work with us, not against us. Don't shop around endlessly. If you've started working with a mortgage specialist and everything is progressing well, stick with them and ask if they can adjust the rate. Don't be a "mortgage chaser," jumping from bank to bank, pushing for slightly lower rates just because another institution made a counteroffer.

Personally, I've canceled deals because it's simply not worth our time. Clients like this are focused on saving a tiny percentage difference after we've put in all the hard work. I'd rather lose that deal and focus on customers who appreciate the effort we put into their files.

There are many excellent mortgage specialists who can help you with approval, but please, don't waste our time. If you feel the rate we've offered is too high, just ask what we can do and work with us to find a solution. A difference of $20 per month in your payment won't make a significant change for you but can have a long-term impact on us.

Lawyer Percent Ownership: A Tip for Buyers

When purchasing a property, your lawyer will ask how much ownership percentage you will hold, especially if you're buying with others. Here's a small tip: if you don't fully trust your co-owner, whether it's your spouse or a friend, you might consider giving them a lower percentage of ownership. However, keep in mind that if you later decide to remove them from the property, you will be required to pay land transfer tax on the percentage of ownership you're taking over.

For Clients and Industry Professionals (Including Mortgage Specialists)

Please send us one email or one text message—**not** 30 individual messages with one word or sentence each. Before hitting "send," double-check to ensure you've covered everything you need to communicate. We typically don't review those scattered messages until the end of the day.

CHAPTER 10: IF UNDERWRITERS ARE READING ONLY

Dear Underwriters,

We truly appreciate you, but let's be honest—we know more than you might think. Please don't be too hard on us. Our goal is to help people achieve their dreams while also helping the bank make money. We are well-versed in the policies, so when you respond as if we're unaware of something, it's not always the case. Sometimes, we may *pretend* not to know, at least some of us, to avoid disclosing extra information that could work against the file.

So, the next time you're about to send an emotional email, take a moment to consider how long that mortgage specialist has been in the sales force. It's possible that what seems like an oversight was intentional.

Apologies to the general readers—only those working in this industry will fully understand.

Here's a more polished and professional version of your text:

Also, please try not to be too hard on us—we're doing our best to make things happen. Requesting additional documents is often necessary, but sometimes we have to ask: is it really needed? Many of us don't sleep well, and some of us retire early, all because we live and breathe each deal—at least, the professional mortgage specialists do.

We believe in the bank and in our ability to get deals done, but when we're faced with rejections or endless back-and-forth, it takes a toll. We're commission-based, and we fight hard to get to where we are, but it often comes at the cost of our health. So, help us out, and maybe we can make it to our 50s without a heart attack.

CHAPTER 11: FOR DEAR FRIENDS FROM FRAUD DEPARTMENT, IF YOU ARE READING THIS BOOK

Nothing, burn in hell. The end. All information in this book is fictional and made up to impress the reader. All events are made up or purely coincidental.

CHAPTER 12: IF YOU ARE GOING TO DIVORCE OR REMOVE BORROWERS FROM THE MORTGAGE

This is an interesting and common topic in Canada: don't buy property with people you trust implicitly. In Canada, marriage is often treated as a business partnership, and when people approach it this way, it can be difficult to build a wealthy and happy family. So, what happens when you divorce and this is your matrimonial home? It doesn't matter if only one of you is on the title and mortgage—after six months, you both equally own the property. This means one of you will either have to buy out or pay the other 50% of the ownership.

This process can be frustrating, but it happens. Typically, one of the borrowers will come to the branch wanting to keep the property, meaning they need to refinance to remove the other borrower and pay them their share. The issue is that when we remove the second borrower, a full refinance is required. This includes income verification, a credit report review, and other documentation. It's not a simple or easy process, and we often find that the borrower who wants to keep the house may not have a strong enough income. In most cases, they'll end up having to sell the property, unless their partner is generous enough to continue owning it jointly, but that's rare.

Before you rush to refinance and take out equity to pay off your partner, consult with your mortgage specialist to see if it's feasible. Otherwise, selling may be your only option. Yes, there are creative mortgage specialists who can work wonders, but you need to ask yourself if it's worth it and whether you can manage the payments. Don't rely solely on a "magic" mortgage specialist to solve your problem. If you're short on income, there may still be time to address the issue. We could look for ways to increase your income or, if necessary, add family members as co-borrowers to assist with the refinance, but this can get complicated.

In the end, if you're living with a spouse who isn't on the title (registered on the land search portal) or the mortgage, but it's your primary residence, both parties still have 50% ownership. If it's an investment property, it will need to go through a lawyer. However, if it's held under a holding corporation, how would they find out about the extra investment property—unless you disclose it? In this case, silence is truly golden.

If you want to remove a friend from the mortgage, it's definitely possible. The process is similar to refinancing, but without breaking the term. It can be complicated, but it's achievable. One borrower can retain the rate and term while releasing the other from liability. Just like in a refinance, we need to determine whether you qualify to support the mortgage on your own. If you do, we can move forward with the process.

My advice to you: whenever you buy a property and want to protect your equity from potential intrusions, ask a trusted family member or friend to create a numbered corporation and place a charge against your property for the remaining equity. For example, if you have a $500K mortgage and your property's current market value is $1M, you have an additional $500K in equity.

Now, imagine you made a regrettable decision—perhaps you got drunk last Friday and made your spouse's life more miserable by sending their personal photos to all their friends. As a result, lawyers might pursue you, reviewing your divorce papers or demanding damages. If you fail to act, they may attempt to place a lien on your property. However, they won't be able to, because the first position is held by your mortgage with BMO, and the second position is held by that numbered corporation, which covers the remaining equity. Essentially, this shields your property from external claims—unless they manage to get an exceptional lawyer, which is less likely.

So, having a reliable friend (who isn't planning to leave this world anytime soon) could help you protect your equity from external threats. That said, I could be wrong—it's always best to consult with your lawyer for proper legal advice.

CHAPTER 13: MORTGAGE FOR PROFESSIONALS SUCH AS DOCTORS

Dear Doctors and Resident Doctors,

Congratulations on reaching this milestone in your career—I'm sure it wasn't easy. For doctors, dentists, and lawyers (depending on the bank), there are special mortgage programs where your future earning potential is assumed, even if you're currently earning around $60K per year. Each bank has a different scale, but they are fairly similar, and the assumed income can be quite high. The key question, however, is: do you have the down payment?

If you haven't saved up yet, then it's time to start. You probably haven't read my book yet, but you'll learn that saving monthly is essential. You should begin setting aside money now—whether by investing in stocks or simply saving. **Do not** rush to pay off OSAP or your medical line of credit. Let those debts wait. Remember, **pay yourself first, and creditors later**—this is how you'll be able to retire early.

Consider this: if you have medical debt of $100K-$310K, it could take years to pay off even if your salary is around $225K annually. However, if you buy a property or open a clinic, your investment might appreciate after a year or two, allowing you to either sell or refinance it to pay off your debts. Additionally, your clinic will generate income that can help you pay down your loans faster. So, don't listen to those advising you to pay off loans first—they're mistaken. It would take you years to pay off your loans by just working, whereas you could take a calculated risk with investments and potentially pay them off much quicker.

I'd take the risk—after all, you're already fortunate to have made it this far in medicine. We all know how difficult it is to get into medical school and become a doctor. Also, keep in mind that some banks offer business medical loans that can help you start your own practice. Trust me, it's better to control your own time rather than have someone else control it. While starting your own practice isn't for everyone, it's definitely possible.

Remember, some bank programs allow for a 10% down payment, but limitations do exist. Based on your current salary of around $60K per year, your monthly income before taxes is about $5K. With current mortgage rates in the summer of 2024, a $500K mortgage would have a monthly payment of $2,700. That means more than half of your income is going towards your mortgage alone—not including property taxes, heating, and utilities. So, be cautious about what you can afford.

If interest rates drop to 3% by 2026, your monthly payment will be closer to $2,000, which would be a significant improvement. At that point, you can decide whether renting or owning is more worthwhile. Personally, I would opt for ownership, provided that condominium fees aren't too high. Alternatively, you could gather your friends, buy a house together, and split the profits after graduation—or keep it and rent it out. When you work as a team, you can accomplish far more than you ever could alone.

The same advice applies to dentists, doctors, and lawyers—go out there and take those risks. And if things don't go as planned, don't blame me—you likely missed something along the way.

One thing that still confuses me, though, is why there isn't similar financial support for veterinary doctors. While some support exists, it's not as strong as it is for medical doctors. Perhaps it's because we don't yet have an OHIP-equivalent system for agricultural animals?

CHAPTER 14: SCARY TOPIC FOR MORTGAGE SPECIALISTS, AI TAKE OVER

Mortgage specialists, don't worry—change is coming. Yes, banks will begin using AI tools for mortgage approvals, and there will be some replacement of the traditional mortgage channel. However, AI will not be able to replace the critical thinking and creativity of mortgage specialists. AI machines must adhere to strict rules and regulations, and they cannot navigate the grey areas or bend the laws in the best interest of clients. This is where experienced specialists come in, as they understand how the system works and can identify loopholes to help clients secure approvals.

AI is a valuable tool that mortgage specialists can leverage to their advantage, but it won't fully replace the expertise and human touch in mortgage sales. Banks need to diversify their portfolios to succeed in the long run, and losing their mortgage sales force could impact their market share.

With AI on the horizon, it's important to start preparing. Develop solutions and work on alternative or passive income streams, as AI may impact some of your pipeline revenue but not all of it. If you've been living a lavish lifestyle, it might be time to start saving and investing more prudently.

In summary, while AI will influence the industry, professional mortgage specialists will remain essential. Focus on building alternative income sources to secure your future and avoid the pitfalls that market fluctuations, like those experienced in 2023 and 2024, can bring.

To the bank directors, we all understand that minimizing expenses is a priority, and the introduction of AI is inevitable. While I fully support technology, it's important to learn from past examples—take CIBC's digital branch, for instance. They experienced a decline in sales. The reality is that, regardless of the generation, people need human interaction. It's simply in our nature to engage with others who understand our needs. CIBC's misstep in this direction highlights that fact.

Instead of using AI to replace mortgage specialists and branch representatives, consider designing AI tools that enhance their ability to do their jobs more effectively. The bank that chooses to replace its workforce with AI will likely see a drop in sales. In contrast, banks that focus on equipping their teams with AI-driven tools to improve efficiency and performance will thrive.

CHAPTER 15: FOR THE GOVERNMENT AND THEIR HOUSE CRISES

Offering people mortgages for free—just imagine! Bankers' hair would stand on end, and smiles would stretch across the faces of homeowners. Of course, this isn't happening in Canada anytime soon, likely not for the next 300 years. But eventually, the banking system will change, transitioning from capitalism to something more like communism. And ironically, it will be the result of the very system banks helped build. History teaches us this, and those who ignore or fail to understand history are destined to lose.

The government cannot afford to buy all the mortgages from banks to provide people with mortgage-free homes. Doing so would only lead to more borrowing, especially since Canada's GDP is not high enough to support such a move. Given this, we are at a crossroads, and unfortunately, many individuals and companies won't be happy with the available options.

The mortgage industry thrives on speculation and quick profits. Brokers and others involved in the sector are unlikely to let go of this dynamic—at least for now. Ultimately, real change will come when citizens demand it, and when they are ready, the change will happen.

First, eliminating stress tests would allow people to qualify for mortgages at a standard rate, and income fraud would diminish as a result.

Second, why not create a government-run MLS system? Each province already has its own platform for title searches, so a government MLS portal would make sense. Real estate professionals might not like this, but it would put an end to price speculation. Property would no longer be treated as a bargaining chip but rather as an asset meant for people to live in. This could prevent the intentional inflation of purchase prices and reduce the national debt within the mortgage sector by keeping home prices within a reasonable range. In doing so, we'd address two major issues with one solution.

Thirdly, we need to provide more support for first-time buyers who are Canadian citizens. These are the people who will stay in Canada to work, build families, and contribute to the nation's future. Without adequate support, we risk losing Canadian culture. With high interest rates and excessive bureaucratic regulations, young families are hesitant to start, and even when they do secure property, it becomes harder for them to grow into full-sized families with children. This may align with certain government objectives, but if we look at the long-term—rather than the short-term, as the government often does—the more Canadians we have, the more innovation and progress we can generate. And no need to worry about resources, because as we cultivate a more educated nation, we will naturally focus on bigger goals, like space colonization and other advancements.

The government should create a program specifically for the younger generation to help them with down payments. There was a program where you could put down 5% and the remaining 15% was provided through insurance, but the rules and regulations were not designed with people in mind. Those who designed it were so disconnected that only a limited number of people could qualify. It makes you wonder, is this government working for us or against us? It seems more likely they're working against us. They put on a show, claiming to do something great for

Canadians, but in reality, most people never even use these programs. And let's not forget, it's practically a lottery—you might not even get it. I started one application but never managed to finish it due to disqualification, and since then, I haven't had a single client ask about the program.

Fourth, eliminate the principal and interest payments from mortgages. While this may seem impossible for the government at the moment, it's worth considering. In the USSR, there were no mortgages because the government took care of its people, and property ownership rested with the individuals, not the banks, as it does here in North America.

There are many great ideas we could implement, but we currently lack the quorum to push them forward. People's focus has shifted to greed or simply trying to keep up with the payments the government has burdened us with.

Take a look at countries with strong economies. A smart approach is when the government takes control of resources like oil and minerals, ensuring the profits are reinvested back into society— whether that's building new playgrounds for children, increasing hospital beds, or improving social support, as was the case in the USSR.

In contrast, in capitalist systems, those profits often go to the board of directors, who then buy multi-million-dollar yachts or luxury cars. So, think carefully, Canadians.

A funny observation: during the standoff between the USA and the USSR, there was one FBI agent assigned to combat drugs, but 20 agents focused on fighting communist propaganda.

EPILOG

So, you've finished reading this book and now have a glimpse into what it's like to be a mortgage specialist in Canada, as well as the long and often complex journey of securing a mortgage—and the reasons behind it. Be sure to check out my upcoming books, which will cover different topics and delve into more interesting events and crazy experiences from the lives of mortgage specialists.

ABOUT THE AUTHOR

John Geld

John Geld is a seasoned mortgage broker with over a decade of experience in Canada's financial sector. Throughout his career, he has navigated a wide range of lending scenarios and witnessed firsthand the changing dynamics of banking practices. His deep understanding of the mortgage industry and its evolving landscape positions him as an expert in helping clients optimize their financial strategies.

John.Geld13@gmail.com

BOOKS BY THIS AUTHOR

Canadians, Don't Get A Mortgage, Get Money For Life

Canadians Don't Get a Mortgage, Get Money for Life

By John Geld

Unlock the secrets to financial freedom with John Geld's groundbreaking guide. This essential book demystifies the mortgage process and empowers Canadians to harness the power of banks as allies, not adversaries. Whether you're part of the working class, middle class, or affluent society, discover tailored strategies to elevate your financial status and create lasting wealth.

Inside, you'll learn how to navigate the intricacies of mortgages, leverage banking systems to your advantage, and employ savvy tricks that can help you achieve your financial desires. Say goodbye to outdated notions of homeownership and hello to a smarter, wealth-building approach to financing.

Join the movement of empowered Canadians taking control of their financial destinies. It's time to get money for life!

www.ingramcontent.com/pod-product-compliance
Lightning Source LLC
Chambersburg PA
CBHW050326230526
45471CB00005B/2376